T0353185

MIRANDA ROSE HALL

Miranda Rose Hall (she/her) is an American playwright and screenwriter based in Brooklyn, NY.

Her plays include *A Play for the Living in a Time of Extinction* (finalist for the 2021 Susan Smith Blackburn Prize), *Plot Points in Our Sexual Development* (finalist for the 2019 Lambda Literary Award in Drama), *The Kind Ones* and *Menstruation: A Period Piece*. Her work has been produced by theatres including LCT3/Lincoln Center Theater in New York, Baltimore Center Stage, the Magic Theatre in San Francisco and Centaur Theatre in Montreal. She has written commissioned works for Yale Repertory Theater, Playwrights Horizons Soundstage, Baltimore Center Stage, Concord Theatricals, and LCT3/Lincoln Center Theater as a Berwin Lee New York London Commissioned Playwright. In 2020, she was honoured with a Steinberg Distinguished Playwright Award. Miranda has written for television on ABC's *Alaska Daily* and Showtime's *American Rust*.

In addition to writing, Miranda is a founding member and artistic leader of LubDub Theatre Co, a New York-based physical-theatre company that animates stories of science, myth and magic. She graduated with her BA from Georgetown University and her MFA from the Yale School of Drama.

Miranda Rose Hall

A PLAY FOR THE LIVING IN A TIME OF EXTINCTION

NICK HERN BOOKS

London

www.nickhernbooks.co.uk

A Nick Hern Book

A Play for the Living in a Time of Extinction first published as a paperback original in Great Britain in 2023 by Nick Hern Books Limited, The Glasshouse, 49a Goldhawk Road, London W12 8QP

A Play for the Living in a Time of Extinction copyright © 2023 Miranda Rose Hall

Miranda Rose Hall has asserted her right to be identified as the author of this work

Cover image by Michael Wharley

Designed and typeset by Nick Hern Books, London
Printed in Great Britain by Severn, Gloucester

A CIP catalogue record for this book is available from the British Library

ISBN   978 1 83904 149 5

CAUTION   All rights whatsoever in this play are strictly reserved. Requests to reproduce the text in whole or in part should be addressed to the publisher.

Amateur Performing Rights   Applications for performance, including readings and excerpts, by amateurs in the English language throughout the world should be addressed to the Performing Rights Manager, Nick Hern Books, The Glasshouse, 49a Goldhawk Road, London W12 8QP, *tel* +44 (0)20 8749 4953, *email* rights@nickhernbooks.co.uk, except as follows:

Australia: ORiGiN Theatrical, Level 1, 213 Clarence Street, Sydney NSW 2000, *tel* +61 (2) 8514 5201, *email* enquiries@originmusic.com.au, *web* www.origintheatrical.com.au

New Zealand: Play Bureau, 20 Rua Street, Mangapapa, Gisborne, 4010, *tel* +64 21 258 3998, *email* info@playbureau.com

USA and Canada: Creative Artists Agency, see details below

Professional Performing Rights   Applications for performance by professionals in any medium and in any language throughout the world should be addressed to Creative Artists Agency, 405 Lexington Avenue, 19th Floor, New York, NY 10174, USA, fax +1 212 277 9099, *email* sam.barickman@caa.com

No performance of any kind may be given unless a licence has been obtained. Applications should be made before rehearsals begin. Publication of this play does not necessarily indicate its availability for amateur performance.

www.nickhernbooks.co.uk/environmental-policy

A Play for the Living in a Time of Extinction was first performed as an online streamed performance for the Baltimore Center Stage 2021 season (Stephanie Ybarra, Artistic Director; Michael Ross, Executive Director), with the following cast and creative team:

NAOMI   Lindsay Rico

Director   Taibi Magar
Scenic and Costume Designer   Clint Ramos
Lighting Designer   Stacey Derosier
Sound Designer   Twi McCallum

The play was commissioned and developed by LubDub Theatre Company (Caitlin Nasema Cassidy and Geoff Kanick, Co-Artistic Directors; Robert Duffley, Dramaturg).

It was developed, in part, with assistance from the Orchard Project (Ari Edelson, Artistic Director), www.orchardproject.com.

6

The original production of *A Play for the Living in a Time of Extinction* directed by Katie Mitchell was created at the Théâtre Vidy-Lausanne as part of the project 'Sustainable Theatre?', conceived by Katie Mitchell, Jérôme Bel and Théâtre Vidy-Lausanne, with the collaboration of the Competence Centre in Sustainability of the University of Lausanne, co-produced by STAGES – Sustainable Theatre Alliance for a Green Environmental Shift (NTGent – Théâtre de Liège – National Theatre of Croatia in Zagreb – MC93, Maison de la culture de Seine-Saint-Denis – Trafó House of Contemporary Arts – Piccolo Teatro di Milano, Teatro d'Europa – Lithuanian National Drama Theatre – Teatro Nacional D. Maria II – Maribor Slovene National Theatre – The Royal Dramatic Theatre, Dramaten, Stockholm – National Theater & Concert Hall, Taipei) and co-funded by the European Union. 'Sustainable Theatre?' includes two shows and a workshop touring in the form of scripts recreated locally.

The play was first performed in the UK at the Barbican Theatre, London, on 26 April 2023, co-produced by Headlong and the Barbican, with the following cast and creative team:

NAOMI   Lydia West

Director   Katie Mitchell
Set and Costume Designer   Moi Tran
Lighting Designer   Bethany Gupwell
Composer and Sound Designer   Paul Clark
Associate Sound Designer   Munotida Chinyanga
Bike Specialist   Colin Tonks
Assistant Director   Francesca Hsieh
Casting Director   Amy Ball

CITIZENS OF THE WORLD CHOIR
Musical Director   Becky Dell
Creative Director   Meg Ella Brookes
and Associate Music Director

The production was subsequently performed at the Belgrade Theatre Coventry (Director: Nyasha Gudo); Shakespeare North Playhouse, Prescot (Director: Nathan Powell); New Vic Theatre, Newcastle-under-Lyme (Director: Ellie Taylor); Theatre Royal Plymouth (Director: Kay Michael); and York Theatre Royal (Director: Mingyu Lin).

Introduction

Miranda Rose Hall's play *A Play for the Living in a Time of Extinction* takes the audience on a life-changing journey to confront the urgent ecological disaster that is unfolding around us. Part ritual, part battle cry, it is a moving exploration of what is means to be human in an era of man-made extinction.

This life-affirming script has been central to catalysing an international experiment in sustainability. In its original form conceived by Katie Mitchell in collaboration with Jérôme Bel and Vidy Theatre an international tour happened where no materials or people moved between touring venues; instead a set of written guidelines were passed to local teams in each touring city.

In its UK premiere directed and conceived by Katie Mitchell for Headlong and the Barbican Centre the production moves off-grid during the performance to integrate a bike-powered electricity system. With the help of a live wattage counter, audiences see a group of cyclists create electricity in real time to power this innovative show.

Following on from its London performances, Headlong and the Barbican Centre explore a unique UK touring iteration of the original European model where there is one centralised blueprint for how to create the show – shared across six cities – and brought to life by entirely new teams; an eco-relay of sorts, eliminating travel as much as possible.

In engaging in this unique process of theatre-making, initiated by Katie Mitchell in Europe, Headlong, the Barbican Centre, our partner venues and freelancers have discovered alternatives, made mistakes and found hope. It has been a feat of national imagination and European collaboration.

April 2023

For Lisa Starling Duffley
(1959–2019)

Character

NAOMI, *a dramaturg, a woman who is afraid of death,
late twenties or early thirties*

Place

A theater

Time

Now

*This text went to press before the end of rehearsals and so may
differ slightly from the play as performed.*

PART ONE

A theater, a bare stage.

NAOMI *enters.*

NAOMI. –

–

–

–

Uh – hi.

–

Hi, everybody.

–

How's everybody doing tonight?
Raise your hand if you're having an okay day?
Okay.

–

Raise your hand if you're having a good day.

–

Good.

–

Raise your hand if you're like 'my life is a searing hellscape
of doom'.

–

Okay.
Thank you for your honesty.

–

So – my name is Naomi.
And I am the dramaturg and a co-founder of ZeroOmissions
Theater Company, along with my long-time collaborators
and best friends
Zoe Martinez-Goldberg and Sarah Khalile.
And as dramaturg,
my role in this company is to research the content of our
plays, to develop new material,

then to deepen the conversation with the audience.
Basically, I get these facts,
I wonder how facts become performance,
and how performance becomes connection.
–

And uhm – I thought we would be presenting our
performance tonight,
which is a kind of
in-your-face
spectacular meditation on the catastrophe of climate change
that we had been touring for the past two years,
and finally brought to the Barbican.
The Barbican.
Which is, obviously, beyond our wildest dreams.
And this was supposed to be the final performance of the tour.
Like the whole tour, actually,
however,
Zoe and Sarah are not here.
Because uhm – about twenty-four hours ago, Zoe's mother fell.
–
–

It was a random accident.
She is fifty-nine.
Her name is Evelyn Martinez-Goldberg.
And she is currently –
uhm –
–

she is dying.
–

In hospital.
–
–
–

And uhm –
Sarah drove Zoe to the hospital,
and I thought that we would cancel the show tonight, but –
last night Zoe calls me frantically from the hospital and says,
'Naomi, you have to go on for us.
Naomi, you have to finish the tour.

Give us an ending that we're in control of,'
and I'm like,
'But I'm the dramaturg. I can't perform.'
And she's like,
'Then do something else.'
And I'm like, 'What?'
And she's like,
'Just tell them what's happening.'
And I'm like,
'What do you mean what's happening?'
And Zoe says,
'My mother is dying.'
And she hangs up the phone.

–
–
–
–

So now you know what's happening.

–
–
–
–

And I uhm –

–

you know, maybe I should start with like a little bit of
background:
so, we founded this theater company after university
and we called it ZeroOmissions
because we wanted to make sure there was
NOTHING LEFT OUT
of the conversation on climate.
And we spent like
two years
developing this show, it's essentially –
it's our only viable show, actually –
and we have poured our BLOOD, SWEAT, and TEARS into it.
It's about the atmosphere!
And the ocean!
And materiality!

And greed!
And cars!
And BP!
And, not to – give away the ending,
but we start the play with like –
a harmless trip to the beach –
and by the end,
we all die.
Everyone dies.
In a sort of – carnival of death.
An – unscientific apocalyptic bacchanal.
–
Set to music.
–
With choreography.
–
And nudity.
–
And to be honest,
for most of my life,
I have been like –
I am the kind of person who, when she meets her enemy,
is like,
ENEMY, I WILL DEFEAT YOU WITH KNOWLEDGE
AND INFORMATION.
I WILL BLIND YOU WITH MY RIGOROUS
RESEARCHED-BASED ACCOMPLISHMENTS.
And so I feel like we took on these
'issues'
from this perspective of like,
TRIUMPHING through the power of spectacle,
and BEATING AN AUDIENCE INTO SUBMISSION,
into ACCEPTING the ERROR OF THEIR WAYS,
with like
3D MAPPING
and
a LOCAL CHOIR
and EXCESSIVE ELECTRICITY,
and actually –

–

I discovered –

that even though I thought I thought about this work

in what felt like a deep and authentic way,

even though I thought my imagination was moving me

into a place of artistic depth,

I didn't realize how I actually *felt* about any of this until I –

okay, so on this one stop on our tour –

at the post-show talk,

which I always facilitate,

this woman raises her hand and is like,

'Have you heard of this book *The Sixth Extinction* by

Elizabeth Kolbert?'

And I say,

'I started it, but I got busy.'

And she says,

'Well, that's not surprising. It's a difficult book.'

I know.

And so OF COURSE I vow to read it that night.

In one sitting.

So I go back, and I get that book,

and I start rereading it,

and I, a woman devoting her life,

or so she thinks,

to talking about this stuff,

starts rereading this book about mass extinction,

about the apocalypse of the Golden Toad,

and the demise of coral,

and the collapse of the rainforest,

and at first I was like,

yup,

yup,

yup,

got it,

uh-huh,

and I mean, it was unnerving,

the information is unnerving,

but it didn't blow my mind,

I mean I learned things,

it's a very well-researched book,
it won the Pulitzer Prize,
I was learning some things about science history,
and that seemed useful,
the book seemed useful,
and then –

–

–

I get to this chapter about these bats –
these Little Brown Bats –

–

and about how they are dying from this horrible disease –

–

and I was –
uhm –
I'm going to get personal here –

–

I was destroyed.
Emotionally.

–

Which is not –
typically –
my reaction to this kind of information,
and I'm like –
WHAT IS HAPPENING.

–

Because, for the record,
I don't even LIKE bats!
But when I read this chapter
about these Little Brown Bats
dying from this awful disease,
for days,
DAYS –
I was walking around
CONSUMED with these bats,
and even THINKING about them made me weep,
BATS!
So I try to do what any like
reasonable dramaturg does,

I research the shit out of it,
then I try to bring it into the show.
So I start researching, re-researching
extinction, and these bats,
I'm like, okay Zoe, hey Sarah,
can we talk about these bats?
So we try to talk about them.
For like – a week.
And I do this research about extinction, and
I bring in all of these lists of species,
and we TRY to add this nuanced conversation about
extinction into our play,
and they do their like
'Zoe and Sarah' thing,
they make a bat extinction installation act,
but it doesn't feel right,
something doesn't feel right,
and I try to tell them,
you know, that's – not quite right,
and they're like,
but we have taxidermy,
and I'm like –
I think it's bigger than the taxidermy,
and they're like,
'But we already have a CARNIVAL OF DEATH, what else
do you want?'
And I'm like –

–
I'm sort of –
I'm at a loss for words,
which is,
unfortunately,
something that happens to me,
and I wish I could have said,
'I don't know exactly what I want, but something's changing
for me.
Something's different for me now.
And I think that maybe, for all of our – efforts –
I think we haven't actually contended in an honest way with

climate crisis –
or at least –
we haven't contended with it in an honest way that can
adequately respond to my –
to the way I feel when I'm paralyzed by a sense of –
grief and catastrophe.'
–

–

I'm sorry that this is sort of uhm –
–

I really haven't slept –
–

And when Zoe and Sarah left last night,
and I was all alone –
–

has uhm –
has anyone ever felt suddenly, unshakably, and utterly
consumed by the fear of death?
–

–

–

–

Well.
I am going to try something.
For you.
Tonight.
With nothing.
Because even though we have lived through a pandemic,
and we are living through a war in Europe,
I think our culture is still struggling
with how to deal with death.
And especially mass death.
And especially mass interspecies death –
–

So I'm just going to try to tell you a few stories tonight.
About some of the things I have been thinking about and
researching in private.
So that none of us has to be unbearably lonely.
Is that okay?

—

This is my team.
They came on board this afternoon.

The cyclists enter and sit on their bikes.

The staff here has been incredible.
They helped me rig up our bikes so that this performance
could take its electricity off-grid.
These fine cyclists will generate all of the electricity for the
lighting and sound.
We won't go above using five hundred watts of energy per
bike, which is basically the equivalent of one lightbulb in
your kitchen at home.
Usually at the Barbican, a play consumes between eighty
thousand watts for lighting, and thirty thousand watts for
sound, which is about a hundred and twenty thousand watts
in all.
But not tonight.
Alright.

She addresses the technicians.

Are you ready?
Let's take the show off the grid.

The technicians turn off the lights.
The auditorium becomes very dark.
The cyclists start pedaling.
We hear the pedaling.
The light that they power gradually flickers on.

PART TWO

NAOMI. Okay, well –

whether or not you choose to engage with the fact that
humans have caused irreversible climate change,
we have.
You have.
I have.
And we are all participating.
Though I will note that some are participating more than
others.
And I'll note that those who are participating the most will
be the least affected.
But more on that later.
–
So let's just set a few uhm – ground rules for the evening:
we are living on the Earth,
we are never outside of nature,
and we are all participating.
And if participating makes you uncomfortable,
I'll say that's something we have in common.
And if you say, 'but I didn't pay money to participate',
I'll say, 'I also wish that money could protect me'.
–
And maybe
let's just take one big breath in,
and a big breath out.
–
Okay.
–
Okay.
–
Extinction.
–

Extinction –

–

I started learning about extinction in primary school.
Like everyone.
Like everyone who has ever seen a dinosaur toy.
My dinosaur's name was Jessica.
I don't even know what kind of dinosaur it was.
A green one.
And my teacher was like,
'These are dinosaurs, and they went extinct.'
And actually, that is a GREAT opportunity to be like,
'Okay, children, who here knows about mass extinction?'
I feel like that teachable moment
is often overlooked,
anyway –
I suppose eventually I learned that some animals were alive,
and then they weren't, and then I basically didn't think about
extinction again until –

–

and maybe this is a great moment to let you know that
I definitely was not good,
whatever that means,
at science.
I was that kid who sat in science class and basically
lost the will to live because she just did not understand what
was happening.
I mean, I wanted to be the kind of kid who understood science,
but it was so many measurements and so many formulas,
and all of it felt so utterly pointless,
and so basically everything I know about science, I've had to
teach myself as an adult.
And really –
okay, if I just plunge us into the bowels of extinction without
reviewing creation,
this evening isn't going to work,
so actually, how about we take a moment or two to quickly
review the entire history of the Earth.
Are there any professional scientists in the house?

If yes:

Maybe you could like –
gently forgive me.
Okay.
So, this is my like ad hoc version of the creation of the earth
and of its past extinctions according to Western science so
that we can like – get in the zone.
Okay.
–
–

Once upon a time, there was no space.
Then all of a sudden,
there's a lot of space.
The Big Bang.
And out of that space comes gas and dust.
And the gas and the dust become stars.
And one star in particular forms,
a very big star:
the Sun.
More dust and gas become uhm
meteorites and rocks.
They collide!
And become the Earth.
And the Earth is balanced.
And perhaps we could say
that the Earth is neither
happy, nor unhappy,
but it is balanced.
And out of the rock comes gas.
And the gas cools.
And becomes water.
And it RAINS.
CAN YOU BELIEVE IT?!
It RAINS!
This is a major fucking event.
And the water flows ALL OVER the Earth.
And so life begins to form.
Very small life.

Single cells.
And the Earth basically hangs out like this for billions of years.
UNTIL!
Some uh – bacteria – form –
and somehow invent photosynthesis –
which means that they invent OXYGEN.
And THIS is a big deal so...
more things happen.
And somehow,
single-cell organisms start to live collectively,
start to form a like
little cell communes
and turn themselves into species.
Like, super-basic species.
Who don't even hunt.
Who just float around in the water and let all of their food
come to them.
Jealous.
So let's try something – could you all just uh –
make some like
floaty early-species hands?
Or as one of my favorite scholars Donna Haraway might say,
'critters'?
Could you make some floaty early-critter hands?

NAOMI *holds her hands up like critters and shakes them
gently. She gets the assembled to do the same.*

Nice, eh?
And so we are early critters, and there is a burst of life.
Can I get a burst?

The audience presents a burst of life.

So there is a burst of life, and plants start to migrate from the
water to the land, and form these little mossy rock plants.
And these little mossy rock plants process minerals in a whole
new way,
which basically changes everything about the chemistry of
the Earth,
let's keep these critters going –

and so there's global warming and global cooling,
and the species more or less can't keep up with these rapidly
changing conditions, and so we have
MASS EXTINCTION NUMBER ONE.
And most of the critters die.

NAOMI *instructs the critters to die.*

Sorry.
But a couple of the critters randomly survive!

NAOMI *points to some audience members or sections of
audience that are far apart from each other.*

So like – you, and you?
Yup, could you please randomly survive?
Thank you.
So you are the tiny critters who randomly survive, and you
basically – pave the way for life on Earth to keep going.
Well done.
So life on Earth keeps going,
and on my list of notes, I wrote –
'trees'.
So, after the first extinction, TREES, the first TREES
develop. In fact, could you –
since you're warmed up,
would you mind just briefly performing the very first tree to
have ever lived?
You just have to do one interpretive gesture
like
this
or
this
or
this –
and actually, that is so beautiful.
Are there other people who would be willing to perform the
very first trees?
Would anyone be willing to
actually join me on stage and we could like –
maybe sort of dance –
the very first trees to have ever lived?

*She invites some audience members onto the stage. They
perform the first trees to have ever lived.*

Ladies and everyone,
the very first forest.
Thank you.
You can go back to your seats.

They do.

So there are trees,
and then there's another deadly cocktail of events,
which aren't entirely clear but likely involve
temperature changes and maybe volcanoes and maybe
a comet, and so we get a SECOND MASS EXTINCTION.
And how do we even know about any of this?
We know about it from the fossil record, which is
incomplete, but it's basically like –
there are some rocks that are REALLY FUCKING OLD.
And they have stored like – LOADS OF INFORMATION,
there are DEAD PLANTS and ANIMALS and MINERALS
in these rocks,
like they lived near the rock, and when they died, their
bodies were absorbed in the rock,
and bajillions of years later, they're visible in one layer of
the rock,
and then they stop being visible in other, later layers of that
rock –
which is to say that the evidence of life is gone.
And so that's what scientists call extinction events:
the evidence and then total disappearance of life.

–

–

Anyway.

–

So where were we.
The second extinction.
And life starts up again.
And... the continents move.
Did you remember that the continents moved?
I ALWAYS forget that the continents moved.

Sort of like I ALWAYS FORGET
that countries are a recent development.
So anyway, the land of the Earth is moving,
and it forms one MASSIVE continent: PANGEA.
And all this movement changes the climate,
makes it very very hot,
like WAY TOO HOT, sound familiar?
And volcanoes get going –
Carbon dioxide explodes into the atmosphere, there's toxic gas,
the ocean acidifies,
SOUND FAMILIAR?
And we get the MOTHER-LODE extinction,
MASS EXTINCTION NUMBER THREE,
the PERMIAN Extinction,
which we call THE GREAT DYING.
THE.
GREAT.
DYING.
NINETY-SIX PERCENT OF ALL SPECIES DIE.
–
–
–

Hold on.
I need to take a water break.
–
–
–

You know, my mum once came downstairs to the kitchen
when I was a little kid, and found me standing in the dog's
water bowl,
shoving my fingers into the electrical outlet.
–
She put an end to that one really fucking fast.
And I'm sure I can't even tell you
how many times my life has been saved.
–
–
–

Our dog's name was Geranium,
and she slept at the foot of my bed every night,

I loved her with all of my heart,
and I went away for an overnight trip,
the first time I went to Paris, actually,
on the Eurostar,
I went with my aunt,
and somehow Geranium got into something,
and when I came back, Geranium was gone –
–

And my mum told me what happened,
so I knew intellectually that she was dead,
but still I spent a few weeks looking for her everywhere.
Looking for her at the foot of my bed,
looking for her by my bedroom door,
looking for her in the kitchen,
and I couldn't find her anywhere.
And I couldn't wrap my mind around it.
She was there.
And then she wasn't.
And I was terribly sad,
but it somehow felt even worse to be so terribly – confused.
–

–

So anyway.
The apocalypse.
–

–

And afterwards,
the Earth is still around.
Because,
I should point out,
that in all of this,
the Earth does not die.
I don't know if we can say that it is happy or unhappy,
but the Earth
does not die.
And as elements change in the atmosphere
over millions and billions of years,
the Earth just like –
gathers them into itself.
Oxygen,

hydrogen,
carbon.
Because carbon is something the Earth knows how to
deal with.
And it deals with it slowly.
It stores the carbon inside of itself.
Like a mother.
It transforms the carbon until it can rest
inside of itself.
Like a mother.
And when we extract it from the earth,
when we wrench it out of its mother's body –
but I am getting ahead of myself.
–
–

So anyway.
The apocalypse happens –
and then it begins to rain.
And it rains and it rains and it rains.
IT RAINS FOR ALMOST TWO MILLION YEARS.
That's fucking insane.
–

And this is where a lot of
GIANT FLORA AND FAUNA come in.
And then, a mass extinction.
MASS EXTINCTION NUMBER FOUR,
and once again we're not totally sure what happened,
but the basic idea:
Alive.
Dead.
And then somehow DINOSAURS
DOMINATE the Earth!
Hey, Jessica!
And the dinosaurs dominate the Earth UNTIL
an asteroid strikes the Yucatán Peninsula in Mexico,
triggering massive tsunamis.
MASS EXTINCTION NUMBER FIVE.
And Jessica dies.
–

But after she dies, life recovers again.
Because life keeps recovering.
New things evolve pretty quickly.
We get to monkeys,
and monkeys evolve into early humans.
More or less.
Our ancestors.
And we discover happiness and unhappiness,
and we find it very dissatisfying.
We want to eat.
And we want to express ourselves.
We're hunted
and we hunt.
And at first, we are NOT GREAT at staying alive.
But we develop important skills.
And we start to disperse.
We migrate all around the world.
And eventually, we start playing our greatest-known party
trick: killing other species faster than they can reproduce.
For large mammals, you see, it's like this:
it takes a certain amount of time to prepare the body to have
a baby.
It takes a certain amount of time to conceive a baby.
It takes a certain amount of time to give birth to the baby,
and let the baby grow up,
and teach the baby how to be
and if we kill other species before they have time to
reproduce, then the species go extinct.
And sometimes it happens quickly,
and sometimes it takes a very long time.
BUT WHAT IS TIME?!

–

Time can be this:
the distance between two things.
Here I am.
There you are.
I walk to you.

She does.

That is time.
And that is basically human time.
And geologic time is deep time.
Isn't that an incredible idea?
Deep time.
I want deep time.
–

So maybe deep time looks like this:
you are there.
I am here.
And somehow, over a billion years,
we arrive at one another.
–
–
–

We can also understand time as a body.
The body of a tree tells time in rings.
The body of a rock tells time in lines.
Millions of years can condense themselves
into little lines in massive rocks,
lines as thin as cigarette paper.
BUT WHAT IS TIME?!
For humans, perhaps we know it like this:
time is our lifetime.
Time is hours and seasons and phases of the moon.
Time is how long a loved one is alive.
For humans there are maybe
thirty generations in one thousand years.
So there's me,
and my mother,
and her mother,
and her mother,
and her mother,
and her mother,
and her mother,
and her mother,
and her mother,
and her mother,
and her mother,

and her mother,
and her mother,
and her mother,
and her mother,
and her mother,
and her mother,
and her mother,
and her mother,
and her mother,
and her mother,
and her mother,
and her mother,
and her mother,
and her mother,
and her mother,
and her mother,
and her mother,
and her mother,
and her mother,
and all of the species who kept them alive,
all of the plants,
the animals,
the water,
the air,
the land, the atmosphere,
everything they saw,
and touched,
and smelled,
everything they ate,
everything they walked on,
all of existence when they were alive,
that is one thousand years.
–

And to humans, that is deep time.
–

But to the Earth –
let's take that unit,
one thousand years,
then repeat it fifty times,

fifty thousand years,
and that's how long modern Homo Sapiens
have been walking on this Earth.

–

And compare that to the
BILLIONS OF YEARS
that there wasn't even
OXYGEN ON THIS PLANET.
Then compress all of that
into a line in a rock,
as thin as cigarette paper.

–

–

–

–

–

Given that we are,
in the scheme of time,
so totally insignificant,
let's talk about the Sixth Extinction.

–

–

–

The Sixth Extinction is a mass extinction happening right now.
We are living in the midst of a major mass extinction,
and our planet is experiencing the largest loss of life since
the time of the dinosaurs.

–

And another way to say all of this is that we are experiencing
a crisis of biodiversity.
Which is a global emergency.
Because diversity in an ecosystem is THE INDICATOR of
health.
And it is hard to comprehend –
it is hard to wrap your head around the fact that in the last
fifty years –
in my mother's lifetime we have lost – the Earth has lost –
more than two-thirds of its wildlife.
More than two-thirds.

And scientists have determined that the current rates of
extinction are faster, are EVEN FASTER than they were for
the largest mass extinction currently on record, the Great
Dying, which, I'll remind you, wiped out ninety-six percent
of earthly life.

–

And this terrifies me.

–

This information makes me want to crawl in a hole and hide.
But I can't just crawl in a hole and hide because I have to
take some responsibility.
Because unlike past extinctions,
this one is the responsibility of one species,
the most invasive species ever to inhabit the Earth:
Homo Sapiens.
In fact, in the last TWO HUNDRED YEARS,
which is nothing,
IT IS NOTHING
in the SCHEME OF THE EARTH,
in this SPECK OF NOTHING,
human industrial activity and human overconsumption have
so transformed the land and the water
and the air on our planet
that we have entered
a NEW MASS EXTINCTION EVENT.
SO PROFOUND
is our manipulation of this planet
that we have created A SIXTH MASS EXTINCTION EVENT.

–

–

And you may be asking how, how did this happen,
how could anyone let this happen,
and of course the answer is complicated,
but it feels really important to talk about the fact
that even if we, if humans, are the
apex species
in this particular moment of the planet's history,
we need to acknowledge
that there is an apex within the apex –

–

–

Because it is *not* all people.
It is *not all people*.
Not now, not ever.
There is disproportionate participation in the generation of emissions,
and disproportionate suffering on account of those emissions,
and the people who emit, and the people who suffer aren't the same people.
There are gaps in geography and race and economics,
and perhaps the most painful thing about any of this
is that it just did not –
it did not have to happen –

–

I mean, maybe there has never been
a harmonious relationship
between all humans,
or – between humans and the world around us,
but comparatively – ecologically – there was a sort of balance –

–

But it seems like that balance really started to change –
globally –

–

with this world-altering concept
of a hierarchy of race –

–

when Europeans invented this –
system –
in which white Europeans
would have
dominion over the Earth
and People of Color would stop
being people –
would start being
commodities –

–

and –

this system –
which would come to be called
white supremacy
would –
spread all across the globe,
would –
enmesh itself in
law and religion and industry –
would –
motivate
human and ecological
genocide
in order to
accelerate all of these
economies of extraction –
And what is extraction?
Extraction is –
this belief –
that you can take
without taking care –
that you can take
because the Earth is yours –

–

because you've decided that the benefits of that extraction
are somehow more important than the beings they displace
or drive out or extinguish.
And this –
what is happening today –
is not an accident –

–

It is the direct result
of decision after decision made by people who decided they
should be the top of the apex,
that some beings,
some communities,
some ecosystems,
could be reduced to collateral damage,
could be reduced to
'sacrifice zones' –

–

–

and we can't separate any of this
from the story of the more than two-thirds of wildlife
disappearing because nothing on Earth is separate.
Because nothing on Earth – not life, not death, not crisis, not
extinction –
can exist in isolation –

–

because how we care or do not care for each other
is the measure of how we care for the web of life on Earth,
and that is the story of creation.

–

–

–

–

I'm sorry –
I need to uhm –

–

–

Where are we.

–

–

I had a tree.
On my street.
Growing up.
There were – there are – a lot of trees, actually,
but there was a tree
at the end of our street.
And I called it
'my tree'.

–

And my mum would pick me up,
and let me touch the branches.
The leaves.
Which were soft.
And like this big.
And that is the first part of nature that I ever
deeply,

deeply
loved.
Outside of my family,
which is also part of nature,
not that anything is ever outside of nature.
Does anyone else in this room have a tree that they love
very much?

She ad-libs, as needed, to get someone to participate and tell
her a story about a tree. Perhaps she asks questions like:
Who is the tree you love? Where was it? What do you
remember about it? Why did you love it? Is it still there?

Once she has received a story, she thanks the person who
has told her the story.

Has anyone else loved a tree?
Or a mountain?
Or a body of water?

She ad-libs, as needed, to get people to participate. When there
have been enough stories, she concludes the conversations.

Thank you.
–

Uhm –
It is beautiful to hear these stories.
–

I uh – I feel like I have been struggling to find beauty.
And just – struggling in general.
–

A few weeks ago, I went to go see a psychic,
because I thought she might be able to
help me –
and this healer's practice
is to talk to your ancestors,
and we sit in silence for a moment,
and then she says to me,
'Who is Eva?'
And I say,
'That's my mother.'
And she says,

'Why am I getting kitchen?'
And I say,
'I don't know. My mother hates to cook.'
And she says,
'I'm getting a kind of old-fashioned kitchen...'
–

And she's quiet for a minute.
–

'I'm getting an old-fashioned kitchen with a little girl.'
–

And I say,
'Well, when my mother was nine,
she came home from school one day
and found her mother dead in the kitchen.
No one was there to help her.'
–

'That's it,' she says.
And she's quiet for a minute.
–

She says,
'You're carrying that trauma in your root.'
–

And when she says this,
something in me
lunges forward in recognition.
She extends her hands towards me,
and says that she can feel it.
That trauma writes itself onto the atoms of our bodies,
and it changes our atoms,
and our DNA.
And we pass this along to each other,
and what we inherit is out of our control.
And when I was born,
my body was carrying
my mother's memory
of her mother's death,
and maybe all I can say is that when I look at the trauma of
extinction, something at the root of me can recognize itself.

PART THREE

NAOMI. Okay.
So.
The difference between death and extinction is this:
death is to cease to exist.
Extinction is to extinguish.
I now think of death as individual.
Extinction is collective.
One death is not an extinction.
But it can be part of an extinction,
and in some cases,
it can be the very final death,
in which case it is
total extinction.
–
–

The International Union for the Conservation of Nature has
a list of all of the species who are threatened by extinction.
They call this list the Red List of Threatened Species.
There are currently over a hundred and fifty thousand species
on the Red List.
The species threatened with extinction include
forty-one percent of amphibians,
thirty-seven percent of sharks and rays,
thirty-six percent of reef-building corals,
thirty-four percent of conifers,
twenty-seven percent of mammals
and thirteen percent of birds.
All of these are conservative numbers.
I downloaded some images of some of these species,
because I didn't know what they looked like,
and I wanted to see them,
and even though I can barely pronounce some of their
names, forgive me,
I would like to share some of them with you.

NAOMI *begins her slideshow.*

Of Least Concern:
The Alpine Marmot
Western European Hedgehog
European Beech
European Water Vole
Crested Lark
Peacock Butterfly
Pennyroyal
Eelgrass
Bitter Willow
Holly
Hazel
Stoat
Common Kingfisher
Common Starling
–

Near Threatened:
Garden Dormouse
Common Ash
Tiger Shark
European Pond Turtle
Dartford Warber
Woodland Grayling
Giant Australian Cuttlefish
Bongo
Swordfish
Curlew Sandpiper
Red-Legged Partridge
Atlantic Halibut
–

Vulnerable:
Horse Chestnut
Common Stingray
European Turtle-Doc
Lesser White-Fronted Goose
Atlantic Cod
Snowy Owl

Sperm Whale
Common Spiny Lobster
Walrus
Haddock
Sharp-Tailed Sandpiper
Polar Bear

–

Endangered Species:
Basking Shark
European Rabbit
Herefordshire Whitebeam
White Skate
Lemon-Colored Antrodiella
Golden Snub-Nosed Monkey
Enchanting Paphiopedilum
Tucuxi
Little Brown Bat

–

Critically Endangered:
European Sturgeon
Cornish Path-Moss
European Eel
Slender-Billed Curlew
Horrid Ground-Weaver
Marbled Gecko
Derbyshire Feather-Moss

–

Extinct in the Wild:
Socorro Dove
Wyoming Toad
Père David's Deer
St Helena Redwood
She Cabbage Tree
Golden Skiffia
Christmas Island Blue-Tailed Shinning-Skink

–

Extinct –

–

And you know,
I tried to compile a list of species that have gone extinct
during my lifetime because I was alive when they
disappeared,
therefore I somehow participate in that responsibility,
but you know what,
it is really really hard to say when, exactly when
a species goes extinct,
because it's not like they just
leave you a note on the kitchen table saying,
'Hey, I'm going extinct,'
they just start dying,
and then they're gone –
–
–

And there are people all over the world who are doing
everything they can to stop what is happening,
they are devoting their lives to restoration and conservation,
they are putting their lives on the line for clean water and
clean air – and still –
–

during the twenty or so years that I have been alive on this
Earth –
–

here is a partial list of the species that have been declared
extinct in my lifetime:
Aldabra Brush-Warbler, declared extinct 1994
Saudi Gazelle, declared extinct 1994
Kauai Oo, declared extinct 2000
Mount Glorious Torrent Frog, declared extinct 2002
Cyanea Dolichopoda, which might have grown in just one
extraordinary place in Hawaii, declared extinct 2003
Golden Toad, declared extinct 2004
Eiao Monarch, declared extinct 2006
Pinta Giant Tortoise, declared extinct 2012
Christmas Island Pipistrelle, declared extinct 2016
Splendid Poison Frog, declared extinct 2018
–
–

and these species are not disappearing in isolation,
no life exists in isolation,
we are part of a web of life,
and when we lose – when we permanently lose a part of that
web –
the entire web feels it –
however consciously or unconsciously,
there is no such thing
as death in isolation,
because – because like when I was a little girl,
we used to go to the Lake District every summer,
and I realized,
when I went back this summer, that there were all of these
midges,
like more than I ever remembered,
and I was like – really pissed,
like really pissed
and my aunt was like –
well, of course there are more midges
there are fewer bats,
and I was like –
oh my God –
the Little Brown Bats –

–

–

the Little Brown Bats,
an endangered species,
with their glossy brown fur,
and their mouse-ears,
and their nose –
the Little Brown Bats,
who, for a very long time,
lived peacefully,
until several years ago,
when a devastating disease called white nose fungus
started to appear.
A disease with no known container,
whose range is spreading every year,
a little white fungus started to appear,

on the Little Brown Bat noses,
and the people who saw it didn't know what it was.
They just saw bats with white noses.
But soon they noticed
that the bats were disappearing, their numbers were
dropping, and people started saying,
'Where are the bats?'
So scientists start walking into caves where the bats are still
living,
hibernating,
and what do the scientists find?
Piles and piles of dead bats.
Bats who don't wake up from hibernation.
Piles and piles and piles of bats,
DEAD BATS,
ALL OVER THE CAVE,
with little white noses,
ALL OVER THE CAVE.
And they see some bats waking up from hibernation,
and SOME OF THESE BATS just DIE RIGHT AWAY,
some wake up and drop dead,
bats with white noses,
and some bats wake up and try to fly out of the cave,
but they DIE as soon as they start to FLY,
because they are DEHYDRATED,
and OTHER BATS wake up,
and they FLY TO THEIR FRIENDS,
THEIR MATES,
THEIR FAMILIES,
these PILES OF BATS,
and the living bats go,
WAKE UP! WAKE UP!
WAKE UP! WAKE UP!
WAKE UP! WAKE UP!
WAKE UP! WAKE UP!
WAKE UP! WAKE UP!
WAKE UP! WAKE UP!
WAKE UP! WAKE UP!
WAKE UP! WAKE UP!

–

–

–

But they DON'T WAKE UP.

–

Because the BATS ARE DEAD.
Asphyxiation!
Dehydration!
Heartbreak!
DEAD DEAD DEAD!

–

–

–

–

Are you feeling this – this level of panic?
It feels like everywhere I look is a wound.
I am so overwhelmed by these rates of death,
as if this scale of violence were somehow unavoidable,
as if brutality were inevitable,
as if brutality were not a choice,
as if choices were not human,
as if what is human could never be changed,
as if it were inevitable –
it isn't inevitable –
I feel like it is a failure of individualism,
a failure of imagination,
a crisis of death outpacing birth,
of violence outpacing restoration,
of the myth of disposability outpacing the truth of a shared
ecology,
of interconnection,
and why do I care?
Because I don't want to be the only one alive amidst the
dying,
because I don't want to live in a world that's missing so
much life,
because I don't want to wake up one morning
after a very long sleep
and find my mother dead in the kitchen

from disease, or heartbreak, or human indifference,
I don't want my mum to die –
or my aunts or my cousins or my neighbors to die,
I don't want there to be sacrifice zones –
–

And I know that I need to make peace with death,
I know I need to make peace with mortality,
but I can't –
I can't –
make peace with mass extinction –
I can't make peace with mass extermination,
there has to be a different way to be living,
there has to be another way to be human,
I want to live for something more
than the total extinguishing of life –
–

–

and Evelyn Martinez-Goldberg,
mother of my best friend Zoe,
who has brown hair,
and green eyes,
who has three children,
and one ex-husband with whom she is on
extremely good terms,
Evelyn Martinez-Goldberg,
who sent me a special note of condolence
when my Grandfather Jimmy died
who always said that our productions were great
and donated fifty pounds each year,
Evelyn Martinez-Goldberg,
who wasn't supposed to die today,
who is dying in her hospital bed,
I wish you a good death.
–

I hope you are calm.
I hope you are held.
I hope you are smelling your daughter's hair.
I hope there is music in your room.
I hope you feel at home in yourself, surrounded by love.

–

Evelyn Martinez-Goldberg,
and all of the beings dying around you:
the bats and the frogs and the fish and the trees and the reefs
and the bugs and the birds and the people –
all creatures whose mothers are dying, all mothers, all beings
who have ever given life –
I wish you good deaths.
In spite of great odds.
In spite of great cruelty.
And I know I can't change what is happening from this stage
inside of this theater,
but I want to bless you anyway,
and all of the species who have kept you alive,
all of the plants,
the animals,
the water,
the air,
the land,
the atmosphere,
everything you have seen,
and touched,
and smelled,
everything you ate,
everything you walked on,
all of existence while you were alive –
I want to bless this Earth –

–

–

–

And to the living:
to those alive right here with me:

–

I bless you.
And I wish you good deaths.
In spite of great odds.
In spite of great cruelty.
I hope you will be free from harm.
I hope you will feel loved, and held,

and in the meantime –

–

I wish you the peace
to see these deaths
these hundreds and thousands and millions of deaths,
all of this death
as part of our own.

–

How can it be outside of us?

NAOMI *summons a final blessing.*
It begins as something she speaks, and perhaps it ends as
a song.

And before I die,
I want to go home.
I want it to be summer.
I sit with my friends in their beautiful garden.
They offer me a glass of cool, cool water.
We are facing west.
The verge across the street is overgrown,
and we hope that no one mows it.
Wildflowers and wild grasses have sprung up on their own.
We do not know the future, or how it will come.
We do not know how long we will live,
or how children we love will suffer.
We fear for our Earth.
For our city.
For the suffering that has come to pass.
And yet, we are alive –
we sit with so many tensions, and somehow with each other.
We sit and savor the wildness –
we bless –
we bless –
we bless –
we bless life in the final hours of the day –

The song ends. A silence.

The End.

Headlong

We're Headlong. We make theatre with the power to move.

Big, exhilarating productions that use the unexpected to connect everyone we reach, right across the nation. Whether a work is old or new, there are always different questions we can ask. So our productions are an invitation: to come and see something in a new way. Join us.

Previous Headlong productions include *Henry V*, *Jitney*, *Corrina, Corrina*, *Best of Enemies*, *People, Places & Things* and *Enron*, and major digital theatre innovations *Signal Fires* and *Unprecedented*.

www.headlong.co.uk

Staff List

General Manager	Joni Carter
Marketing Manager	Bella Cox
Development Manager	Lucy Howard Taylor
Finance Director	Keerthi Kollimada
Executive Director	Lisa Maguire
Assistant Producer	Radha Mamidipudi
Executive Assistant	Carla-Marie Metcalfe
Development Consultant	Kirstin Peltonen
Literary Manager	Frank Peschier
Producer	Zoe Anjuli Robinson
Artistic Director	Holly Race Roughan
Communities Associate	Iskandar إسكندر R. Sharazuddin

Headlong is grateful for the generous support of the following Trusts and Foundations:

Backstage Trust
The Buffini Chao Foundation

We would like to thank the following individuals for their generous support:

Neil and Sarah Brener
Annabel Duncan-Smith and Victoria Leggett
Alyce Faye Eichelberger-Cleese
Nick Hern Books
Jack and Linda Keenan
Beth and Ian Mill KC
Rob O'Rahilly

We are also grateful for the dedicated support of our Board members:

Justin Audibert
Paddy Dillon
Cas Donald
Sarah Ellis
Lucinda Harvey
Julia Head
Jacqueline Hurt
Prime Isaac
Nicky Jones
Lil Lambley
Donna Munday
Sir Trevor Phillips OBE
Toni Racklin
Lesley Wan

Supported using public funding by
**ARTS COUNCIL
ENGLAND**

barbican

A world-class arts and learning organisation, the Barbican pushes the boundaries of all major art forms including dance, film, music, theatre and visual arts. Its creative learning programme further underpins everything it does. Over a million people attend events annually, hundreds of artists and performers are featured, and more than 700 staff work onsite. The architecturally renowned centre opened in 1982 and comprises the Barbican Hall, the Barbican Theatre, The Pit, Cinemas 1, 2 and 3, Barbican Art Gallery, a second gallery The Curve, public spaces, a library, the Lakeside Terrace, a glasshouse conservatory, conference facilities and three restaurants. The City of London Corporation is the founder and principal funder of the Barbican Centre.

The Barbican is home to Resident Orchestra, London Symphony Orchestra; Associate Orchestra, BBC Symphony Orchestra; Associate Ensembles the Academy of Ancient Music and Britten Sinfonia, Associate Producer Serious, and Artistic Partner Create. Our Artistic Associates include Boy Blue, Cheek by Jowl, Deborah Warner, Drum Works and Michael Clark. The Los Angeles Philharmonic are the Barbican's International Orchestral Partner, the Australian Chamber Orchestra are International Associate Ensemble at Milton Court, and Jazz at Lincoln Center Orchestra are International Associate Ensemble.

The City of London Corporation is the founder and principal funder of the Barbican Centre

www.nickhernbooks.co.uk

facebook.com/nickhernbooks

twitter.com/nickhernbooks